Digital Marketing Basics

Basics

Simplified for fast reading.

30

Minutes

Book series

By Salehe A Nantembelele

Published by:

Create Space Independent Publishing Platform

United State of America

ISBN-13: 978-1548177133
ISBN-10: 154817713X

This page intentionally left blank

To three women I love the most;

Rukia, Fatuma & Amne

Table of Content

CREATE ONLINE PRESENCE

Make A Website & Email Address

If you want to run a Digital business, you have to need a website. People will search your website and when they will get your website, they will be know about your brand, your service and products. Interested customers will contact with you from your website. So a website is essential to run a Digital business.

Strategy:

1. Register a domain name. Domain means your website name. (ex: www.yourwebsitename.com)
2. It will be best if your domain name contains your brand name.
3. Domain name should be small and try not to use numeric character. (ex: www.websitename24.com)

4. Hire a web developer and discuss about an user friendly design.
5. Website must be simple and user friendly. So visitors will get their information shortly.
6. Place a search box into your website.
7. Talk to your web developer about a contact page in your website.
8. Contact page must be enriched with all contact information and address.
9. It will be better if your website is one landing page and website must be responsive. Because one landing page helps to visitor to get information easily and responsive web page is for mobile or tab device. As many people will browse your website from mobile device so responsive design will be helpfull for them.
10. 10. Add product page, service page, our customers, contact page etc.
11. Add social sharing system into your website, so customers can share with others.

Ecommerce Website

E-commerce (electronic commerce or EC) is the buying and selling of goods and services, or the transmitting of funds or data, over an electronic network, primarily the Internet. So if you want to sell your product online, you have to make an ecommerce website or develope your old website into e-commerce website. Your product will be in your website with price, product pictures and details. People will see and if they interested, they will buy. But how they buy? Is there any online payment gateway? If you don't have online payment gateway just talk to your web developer. For an online gateway you may need a license.

Strategy:

1. 1. Make a e-commerce website or turn your old website into e-merce website
2. Enrich your ecommerce website with your products or service.
3. Must be add several image for each product.
4. Mention the product/service price with detail information.
5. It will be better if you add product rating and review option.
6. If you can give a free delivery service that will be awesome.
7. Take a payment gateway license and integrate with your website.
8. Better to add international payment system like paypal, payza, muster card, visa card etc.

Facebook Fan page

Facebook is a social networking website where over 1.25 billion users are active till 2015 and connected with each other. Creating a Fan Page provides your business and brands with another branding outpost on the web where prospects, customers, future employees, vendors, and even the media can find information about your company and the products and services you offer. So If you can reach to them your selling will be increase. So this is essential for a Digital marketing.

Steps:

1. Create a fan page with your company or brand name
2. Add your company logo and an attractive cover photo in your fan page.
3. Enriched facebook About page with company information and contact details.
4. Post your product/service with photo and description.
5. Add your brand's service or product video on timeline.
6. Talk to others and connect your online presence
7. Share with others.
8. Start following people and other company
9. Increase your page like
10. Expand your audience with hashtags

Twitter Branding Page

Every day, millions of people use Twitter to create, discover and share ideas with others. Now, people are turning to Twitter as an effective way to reach out to business. From local stores to big brands, and from brick and motor to internet based or service sector, people are finding great value in the connections they make with business on Twitter. So If you can reach to them your selling will be increase. There are some different types of page in Twitter. You need to create a Branding page for your business.

Steps:

1. Create a branding page
2. Upload your brand logo and cover image.
3. Complete your twitter account profile completely
4. Start following people
5. Talk to others and connect your online presence
6. Share your company's service and products
7. Add your brand's service or product video on twitter timeline.
8. Increase your followers
9. Expand your audience with hashtags

Google+ Business Page

Google Plus was established in the beginning of 2013 as the second largest social network in the world, having over 500 million users till 2015. However, it seems that in this part of the world, no one's really started to feel the presence of this giant yet. When you create a Google Plus page, you create new business opportunities across all of Google's products. From bringing you closer to the top in Google searches, to having a Google map with directions to your store appear when someone types in your brand name, these are not benefits you'll want to miss out on.

Steps:
1. Create your google plus account with gmail id.
2. Add your information to fulfill your profile.
3. Add your page information with profile photo
4. Add an introduction, tag line and contact information
5. Follow other page and talk to them
6. Increase your page follower
7. Post your about your service and products with photo
8. Post a video of your brand's service and product
9. Share with others

Youtube Channel

A youtube channel will be help you to publish your company video and reach to others. More than 1 billion users are in youtube, 300 hours of video are uploading to youtube in every minute. Youtube is localized in 75 countries and every day people watch hundreds of million of hours on youtube. So if your product's video reach to them your selling will be increased.

Steps:
1. Create an account and complete your profile
2. Setup your channel with logo, social icons, color backgrouds, profile information and keyword tags on the page.
3. Upload your brand's service and product video with search friendly video tags.
4. You can create a playlist if you have to upload much video.
5. Subscribe to others channel and share your videos with others
6. You can also share your brand's video in social media like facebook, twitter, google+

Make A Mobile App

One of the biggest benefits of having a mobile app is that all the information you'd like to provide to your customers – including special sales and promotions – is right at their fingertips. Through push notifications you're getting even closer to a direct interaction, and can easily remind customers about your products and services whenever it makes sense.

Why Do You Need a Mobile App for Your Business:

1. 65 percent of U S smartphone shoppers prefer to use mobile apps for shopping.
2. Statistics says in 2017 there could be 200 million downloads of mobile apps.
3. Google play store has reached over 1.5 million apps till 2015.
4. Apple app store has reached over 1.4 million apps till 2015.
5. Microsoft windows store has reached over 500,000 apps till 2015.

So the demand of mobile app is growing up. Just hire a mobile app developer and say him/her to make an app for your business.

SEO

SEO means Search Engine Optimization. Search Engine Optimization is a system by which your website's visitor will be increase because of your website's high ranking placement in the search results of a search engine. I want to clear the concept more. If a visitor go to a search engine (ex: google.com, bing.com, yahoo.com) for searching his/her content, usually he/she types something to the search box. When visitor get the search result usually they go to the link which is in the first position of search result. And 80% people don't go to the 2nd search result page. Because they got their content in first page. So if your website link is in the first page, what about that? More people will come to your page and they will see your product and service. So your selling will be increase rapidly.

Why Do You Need to SEO for Your Business:

1. Your website will may be in the first page of search result.
2. You will get more visitor for your website.
3. More visitor will buy your product or service
4. So your selling will be increase.

Just hire a Search Engine Optimization Professional to make SEO for your website.

SEM

Short for "search engine marketing," SEM is usually used to describe the immediate, money-backed portion of search engine marketing that commonly takes the shape of PPC (pay-per-click)/CPC (cost-per-click) search engine results page ads in one form or another. Simply we can say SEM is a paid advertising system for your website. And this advertisement will be show to the visitor who are searching something relevant of your website/business. And this advertisement shows at search engine. So easily you can get more visitor.

Terms of SEM:

1. Paid search advertising
2. PPC (pay-per-click)
3. PPC (pay-per-call) – some ads, particularly those served to mobile search users, may be charged by the number of clicks that resulted in a direct call from a smartphone.
4. CPC (cost-per-click)
5. CPM (cost-per-thousand impressions) *
6. Most search ads are sold on a CPC / PPC basis, but some advertising options may also be sold on a CPM basis.

Social Media Marketing

Social media marketing is the process of marketing through social media sites like Twitter, Facebook and YouTube. By utilizing the social aspect of the web, social media marketing is able to connect and interact on a much more personalized and dynamic level than through traditional marketing. This type of marketing can often be automated, so it is simple to implement. It can also be very effective for online based companies, and can be a great way to promote a company/business. (ex: If you login to facebook, you will see some ads on the right side of page and some ads on timeline.)

Effective Social Media for Marketing:

1. Facebook
2. Instagram
3. Twitter
4. Pinterest
5. Google+
6. Linkedin
7. YouTube

Mobile App Advertisement

Statistics say, 2 billion smartphone users globally by 2015 and 83% of internet usage from mobile device. 5.13 billion smartphone users globally by 2017. So it is increasing rapidly. And if you can reach them with your product and service, your sell will be increase automatically. To reach them you have to invest for mobile advertisement.

Some Mobile Advertising Company:

1. AdMob
2. Millennial Media

3. Adfonic
4. Chartboost
5. Tapjoy
6. Aditic
7. Admoda
8. Flurry
9. Hunt
10. inMobi

Online Portal Advertisement

Online Portal Advertising is a form of advertising on websites portals that are highly relevant to the advertiser's target market. It uses web banners that are strategically designed and placed on niche websites to entice visitors to check out the services or products being offered. Clicking on a banner directs visitors to the advertising company's landing page.

Web banners have been used by marketers since the beginning of the Internet. Until now, it remains a popular method for directing traffic and turning visitors into customers or clients. The strength of web banners is that even with just a small space, it can deliver a strong message that attracts a high number of sales leads. Online portal advertising is the preferred marketing strategy of many companies because it brings in high-quality traffic and because of its simple yet effective approach.

Strategy:
1. You can contact with an online portal advertising agency for you placing ads
2. You can contact with different online portals directly without agency

3. Effective online portals are: Online News Services, Online exchange sites, Online buy and sell, Online dating sites, Online chating sites, Technology related blogs, Online job sites, Online radio sites, Government portals, Cultural portals, Stock portals, Search portals etc.

Email Marketing

Email marketing occurs when a company sends a commercial message to a group of people by use of electronic email. Most commonly through advertisements, requests for business, or sales or donation solicitation, any email communication is considered email marketing if it helps to build customer loyalty, trust in a product or company or brand recognition. Email marketing is an efficient way to stay connected with your clients while also promoting your business. With email marketing, you can easily and quickly reach target markets without the need for large quantities of print space, television or radio time or high production costs.

Strategy:
1. Consolidating Your Names
2. Build Your List of Email Addresses
3. Develop Your Email Campaign Mix
4. Write Your Emails
5. Choose Your Recipients
6. Send Your Email Blast
7. Process Opt-Outs
8. Process Bounced Emails
9. Follow Up Step
10. Refine and Repeat

SUPER BRANDING

Branding With Models

A renowned model or celebrity can get the attention of people. A model or celebrity can snatch more customer. So if you hire a model or celebrity for branding your company or products it will be very effective. Your sell will be increase very fast.

Tips:
1. Do not hire a model if you have a low budget for business
2. Not so much necessary, if you start a new and small business
3. Do not consume much money for hiring a model

Discount Offer

Offering potential customers discounts on purchases is a way to quickly draw people into your business. Anytime you tell a customer that he can save money, you're likely to get his attention. Discounts don't only help your customers; they also help your business. From increased sales to improved reputation, discounts may be that one ingredient that can bring business success.

Before Discount Offer:

1. Know your current profit margin, markup and breakeven point
2. Calculate the best discount price to still make a profit
3. Prepare a marketing plan to encourage new customers and bring inactive customers back
4. Find out what your competitors are offering and their current pricing
5. Review other options for promoting sales offers without reducing the price
6. Decide how long the sales price will be offered
7. Review your accounts for any regular times of the week, month or year your business has a sales dip.

Offer To Existing Customers

One of the best - and easiest - ways to increase your revenue and profitability is to sell more to your existing customers. Many customers only know about the products they have bought from you. Simply telling your customers about all the products in your range can bring in more business. Look at what your customers have bought before and offer them other relevant goods and services that might be useful. They will see this as good customer care, rather than an intrusive sales pitch.

Strategy:
1. Offer complementary products
2. Offer discount coupon codes
3. Offer similar products they have purchased before
4. Offer free shipping
5. Offer new and fresh product or service

About the Author

Salehe A Nantembelele has a good experience in business from doing business including online businesses in the past 12 years. Currently he is a president of Yuu Company (group of four business units)

Salehe A Nantembelele is a former Executive Accountant of Taris Consult (sister company of Health Focus Ltd) where he worked for two years and lead to tremendous improvement in the business operations of the group company before he joined SUMATRA (Surface and Marine Transport Regulatory Authority) for 5 years.

He has a bachelor of commerce (B.com) specialized in accounting taken from University of Dar Es Salaam Business School (UDBS).

Salehe A Nantembelele is good speaker with rich contents in entrepreneurship and business.

Salehe A Nantembelele is in love with Amne S Issa
– a girl he married in 2014.